Genre   Historical

Essential Question
How do people show inner strength?

THE SECRET ROOM

BY TERRY MILLER SHANNON
ILLUSTRATED BY DARIA PETRILLI

CHAPTER 1

A SPECIAL ERRAND

Liza snuggled into her pillow. Then she screamed and leaped out of bed. She clawed at her cheek.

Charles, Liza's brother, laughed. Charles said to Liza, "It's just a worm, scaredy-cat!"

Liza asked, "Why did you put a worm on my pillow?" Emma, her sister, just giggled. She picked up the worm and carried it to the window. Liza tried to laugh, too, but she couldn't. She hated wiggly, slimy things. Charles and Emma were younger than Liza, but they were bigger, stronger, and braver. They teased Liza with no fear of retaliation.

Liza got back into bed. She knew she should stand up for herself. In her heart, Liza believed Charles and Emma were right, though. She was too small, and she had an infinite number of fears. She just <u>didn't measure up</u>.

> **In Other Words** wasn't as good. En español, *didn't measure up* quiere decir *no fue adecuada*.

Liza

The next day, Liza woke early and helped her mother serve breakfast.

Liza's mother said, "Thank you, Liza girl. I can't believe my daughter will soon be 12. She is getting to be quite the young lady, isn't she, Papa?"

Liza's father smiled and said, "She surely is."

Liza smiled back and began to eat her breakfast. Her parents moved into another room. They spoke quietly. Liza thought her parents were talking about her. Liza tried eavesdropping on her parents. But Liza didn't see Charles sneak up behind her. He slammed two pot lids together.

Liza shouted, and Charles and Emma laughed. Emma gave Liza a hug and said, "Sorry, big sister, but you are so easy to tease."

Liza knew Charles and Emma weren't being mean. But she wished the endless teasing would stop.

Liza went outside. Soon the family would walk together up Main Street. Papa's blacksmith shop was just past the grocery store. Mama, Liza, Charles, and Emma would continue on to their school. Mama was a teacher there. Liza sat on the stoop to wait for the others.

Liza's mother came out and said, "Papa and I think you are old enough now. I need your help with something important."

Liza started to get excited, but she said nothing. Mama continued, "I want you to help me with Free Frank's lessons after school today."

Liza's mother was teaching Free Frank to read and write. Liza knew that Mama did much more out at Free Frank's farm than just teaching reading and writing.

Mama

stoop

town

Free Frank's real name was Frank McWorter. He was the town's founding father, or person who started the town. New Philadelphia was the first town in the United States to be founded by a person who used to be a slave. Free Frank had determination and fortitude. He was slowly buying his children's freedom from slavery, one by one.

Mama often said that Liza's family was lucky to live in New Philadelphia. Mama would say, "Black people and white people live happily together here. You don't often see that."

The basement at Free Frank's farm had thick, concrete walls. In the basement, Free Frank hid people fleeing from slavery. The basement was a stop along the Underground Railroad. The railroad helped slaves travel north to freedom.

Liza's heart beat fast. Liza said, "I'd love to help, Mama."

STOP AND CHECK

Why do Charles and Emma make fun of Liza?

CHAPTER 2

A NEW FRIEND

Liza was distracted and excited all day. She was sure that Mama wanted her to help with Frank's secret room.

After school, Liza and Mama walked to Free Frank's farm. When the time was right, Mama would tell her what was happening. Still, Liza stared at Mama, waiting for her to speak.

Finally, Mama said, "Okay, child, stop looking at me that way. I'll tell you what is going on. You're old enough now to help with the fugitives."

Liza's heart skipped a beat. Liza nodded her head.

Her mother continued, "We're taking shoes to those poor people. They ran away in just their bare feet. Thankfully, our kindhearted shoemakers offered to help. I think some of the fugitives may have to stay here for a while."

In Other Words she was excited. En español, *skipped a beat* quiere decir *estaba emocionada*.

Liza asked why the fugitives had to stay in this place. Mama just pointed at the farmhouse's cellar door. "You'll see," she said.

Liza entered the secret room behind her mother. Liza saw ten people in the room. They were sitting silently, and they weren't moving.

Mama said softly, "Don't worry. It's just me and my daughter, Liza." The people all seemed to be relieved that it was Mama.

A woman whispered, "It's good to see you again, Annie." Liza saw that the woman was pregnant. Mama said, "It looks like that baby might be born very soon."

There was a girl sitting next to the woman. Mama took Liza over to them and said, "Mary, this is my daughter Liza. She's 11 years old, just like you. Isn't that right, Liza?"

candle

Mary

Language Detective | <u>This</u> is a demonstrative pronoun. Find one more demonstrative pronoun on this page.

Liza looked down at her feet. Mama poked Liza with her elbow. Liza quickly lifted her head. She knew Mama's poke meant she should say hello.

Liza smiled at the girl. Mary was short and thin, just like Liza.

Mary whispered, "I'm glad to meet you, Liza." Liza said that she was happy to meet Mary, too. Liza felt that she would remember this moment forever.

On the way home, Liza was excited. She told Mama, "Mary and I are going to be good friends."

Mama smiled but then spoke seriously. "Remember, you cannot talk about Mary to anyone. You hold her life in your hands. You mustn't forget that."

Liza was annoyed and said, "Of course I know that! Mary and I are the same in many ways. Mary likes to read! She secretly learned to read with the children of the plantation owner."

Mama said, "We'll have to bring some books next time." Mama looked at Liza and asked, "What's troubling you, child?"

Liza answered, "Mary's just like me, but she was born into slavery. I never thought about how slaves are like me." Tears ran down Liza's face. "Why was I born free when Mary has to run and hide?" she asked.

Her mother wrapped her arms around Liza. Mama said, "Oh, honey. Sometimes life makes no sense. We just keep doing the best we can."

friends

Mama said, "You'll get to spend some time with Mary. Ruth, Mary's mother, can't travel until she has her baby. It's amazing she got this far."

Liza skipped a little skip. Mary, her new friend, was staying a while, and Liza was excited!

Every day, Liza and Mama visited Ruth and Mary. They brought food, clothes, and books. Mary told Liza about the rigors of her hard life and the dangerous road to freedom. Liza thought that Mary was very brave.

One afternoon, Mary told Liza that they would be best friends forever. Liza shook her head and asked, "Why do you want to be my friend? I'm small and weak. I'm not at all disposed to being brave like you. I'm scared of just about everything!"

Mary laughed and said, "Of course I want you as my friend. We're birds of a feather. We are so much alike. Besides, there are many ways to be brave."

STOP AND CHECK

Why is Liza surprised Mary wants to be her friend?

CHAPTER 3

EMERGENCY!

The next day, there was a big storm. Liza worried that they might not be able to visit the farm. After school, Mama said, "We have to go. Free Frank is taking some people to their next hiding place. Ruth and Mary are alone at the farm."

Liza and Mama had a long, wet walk. At the farm, Mary greeted them. She was crying and said, "Mama's having the baby!"

Liza's mother hurried over to Ruth. After some time, Mama said to Liza, "Ruth needs the doctor."

Liza said, "I'll go, Mama!"

Mama said, "You can't. It's dark and stormy. The doctor is much too far away!"

Liza pulled her coat tight. Liza turned to her mother and said, "I have to do it. No one else can go."

Liza quickly stepped out into the wet, dark night.

The rain was pounding hard on the ground, and it was very windy. The night was black. Liza could barely see her feet. Liza fell into a mud puddle.

Liza was all alone in the mud and rain and darkness. Liza thought to herself, "I can't do this. I'm just a small, weak girl. I'm scared of what might be out there in this horrible night."

Then Liza thought of Mary's mother. Ruth and the baby really needed the doctor. She had to keep going.

Lisa told herself, "The hardest journey always starts with the first step."

Liza got up and kept walking toward town to find the doctor. Soon Liza began to walk faster. Mary's mother and the baby might die. They needed a doctor quickly. Liza began to run. She splashed through the mud and the terrible rain.

This was a difficult night for Liza. She was frightened, frozen, and soaking wet. She felt that she would never reach the doctor's house.

Liza kept thinking of Mary. Her friend's life was hard, but Mary was undaunted. Mary was always courageous and cheerful. "I can be like Mary," Liza thought.

The sky flashed. That did not bother Liza. She forgot that she was scared of lightning. Liza just kept going so she could help her friend.

Finally, Liza reached the doctor. The doctor and Liza rode on Dr. Smith's horse to Free Frank's farm.

Liza thought, "Please let us not be too late." Liza led Dr. Smith into the basement behind the rock wall. Mary's mother cried out when she saw the doctor's face.

Liza's mother calmed Mary's mother down. Mama said, "It's all right, Ruth. He's white, but he's a good man—like many other white people. He's here to help you."

A baby boy was born safely that night. Mary and her mother named the baby Henry. Soon the little family headed north to freedom. Liza missed Mary. Then in the spring, Liza received a letter.

Dearest Liza,
All is well. Mama, Henry, and I are safe and free! Every day we remember Liza, our courageous and strong friend. Thank you for saving Mama and little Henry.
With love from your best friend forever,
Mary

STOP AND CHECK

What did Liza discover about herself during her journey for help?

Summarize

Use important events from
The Secret Room to summarize
the story. Your graphic
organizer may help you.

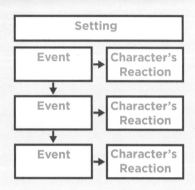

Text Evidence

1. What features of the text tell you this is historical
   fiction? GENRE

2. Why must Ruth and Mary remain at the farm for
   a while instead of making their way to freedom?
   CAUSE AND EFFECT

3. Mary uses part of the adage "birds of a feather flock
   together" on page 10. What does she mean? What
   clues helped you figure out the meaning?
   ADAGES AND PROVERBS

4. Write about the events on page 13–14. How did Liza's
   friendship with Mary help her overcome her fears and
   rush to get the doctor? WRITE ABOUT READING

Compare Texts

Read about a girl who had the inner strength to stand up for what she wanted.

Featherella

peacock feathers

Ella dreamed of traveling to far-off lands. She made herself a dress of turquoise peacock feathers to wear on her travels. Her father thought it was a wedding dress.

Ella's father said, "I've found the perfect husband for you! He's a woodsman, and he's young and strong."

Ella wanted to travel. She didn't want to get married. Ella decided to make it difficult for the woodsman to marry her. "I'll marry the woodsman if he brings me a talking pinecone," she said.

Ella was very upset when the woodsman handed her a pinecone. The pinecone said, "It is my pleasure to serve you."

Ella's father refused to change his mind. One day, Ella put on her traveling dress and sneaked away to the next kingdom. She found a job at the king's castle. She called herself Featherella.

Illustration: Sean O'Neill

Prince Tyrone saw Ella in her beautiful feather dress. He fell madly in love with Ella. The prince begged Ella to love him, too. Ella just ignored the prince. Ella thought the prince only loved her because she was beautiful in her dress.

Ella's job was to care for the royal chickens. She fed the chickens and gathered their eggs. All the time, she dreamed of far-off places.

The queen didn't want her son thinking about the chicken maid. She decided the prince needed to be distracted. Prince Tyrone's favorite food was johnnycake. The queen decided to have a best johnnycake contest. Only young ladies were allowed to be in the contest. The prize was whatever the winner wanted. The winner might even ask to marry Prince Tyrone. There was great excitement in the land.

Featherella decided to win the contest. She picked corn and dried the corn kernels by the fire. Featherella ground the corn and made dough. She patted the dough into a perfect circle. Then she fried it. Her johnnycake was golden and crisp.

travel clothes

Prince Tyrone judged all the johnnycakes himself. The prince bit into Featherella's johnnycake. There was a tiny peacock feather inside it. Prince Tyrone knew at once who had made this cake.

The prince told everyone that Featherella's johnnycake was the winner. Prince Tyrone asked the baker to come forward and get her prize.

You can guess the rest of the story. Featherella decided to marry the prince as her prize, and they lived happily ever after.

Well, that isn't really what happened.

Featherella did get her prize, but it was not the prince. She asked to become the king's mapmaker. Ella would be able to travel the world and make maps for the king. She would earn money so she could travel to far-off lands.

Ella found clothing that was better for traveling than a dress with feathers. Then Ella went to travel to far-off lands. Prince Tyrone gave the feather dress to the girl who had made the second-best johnnycake. The girl and the prince fell in love.

Everyone lived happily ever after.

Make Connections

In *Featherella*, how does Ella use her wits to get what she really wants? ESSENTIAL QUESTION

What do Liza in *The Secret Room* and Ella in *Featherella* teach us about not giving up? TEXT TO TEXT

19

Focus on Literary Elements

Imagery Imagery is when writers describe things in such detail that we can see in our minds what the writer says with words. Imagery helps us "paint a picture in our minds" as we read. These images or pictures help us understand a setting, event, character, or other part of a story.

Read and Find In the story, Liza runs through a storm to get the doctor. This scene is full of rich description; for example, "The rain was pounding hard on the ground, and it was very windy." The words "pounding hard on the ground" and "very windy" help us imagine how the storm must have felt. The author also says that Lisa was "all alone in the mud and rain and darkness." This gives us a clear picture of how Liza felt.

Your Turn

Imagine Liza had to go through a snowstorm to reach the doctor. Work with a partner. Make a list of words and phrases to describe Liza in the snowstorm. Now write a paragraph about Liza going to get the doctor in a snowstorm. Use the words in your list to help describe the scene. Try to help your readers to see, feel, and hear the things you write about.